The Secret Lives of
Brown Bears

by Julia Barnes

GARETH**STEVENS**
PUBLISHING
A Member of the WRC Media Family of Companies

Please visit our web site at: www.garethstevens.com
For a free color catalog describing Gareth Stevens Publishing's list of high-quality books
and multimedia programs, call 1-800-542-2595 (USA) or 1-800-387-3178 (Canada).
Gareth Stevens Publishing's fax: (414) 332-3567.

Library of Congress Cataloging-in-Publication Data

Barnes, Julia, 1955-
   The secret lives of brown bears / Julia Barnes.
     p. cm. — (The secret lives of animals)
   Includes bibliographical references and index.
   ISBN-13: 978-0-8368-7655-0 (lib. bdg.)
   1. Brown bear—Juvenile literature.   I. Title.
   QL737.C27B359   2007
   599.784—dc22   2006034869

This North American edition first published in 2007 by
Gareth Stevens Publishing
A Member of the WRC Media Family of Companies
330 West Olive Street, Suite 100
Milwaukee, WI 53212 USA

Gareth Stevens editor: Gini Holland
Gareth Stevens designer: Kami M. Strunsee
Gareth Stevens art direction: Tammy West
Gareth Stevens production: Jessica Yanke and Robert Kraus

Photo credits: © istockphoto.com: Erik Hougaard p. 8; Natalia Bratslavsky p. 9; Stephen Bonnau p. 10;
© Sandra vom Stein p. 13; Len Tillim p. 15; Karla Hart p. 16; Justin Horrocks p. 18; Sandra vom Stein
p. 19 ; Gert Bukacek p. 20 ; Janny Leung p. 21; Dirk Freder p. 23; Sandra vom Stein p. 25; Bill Booth
p. 28; Vera Bogaerts p. 29. All other images from Westline Publishing Limited.

Printed in the United States of America

1 2 3 4 5 6 7 8 9 10 10 09 08 07 06

Contents

Introducing the Brown Bear

Massive, powerful, and fearless, the brown bear is among the strongest of all animals. This creature lives alone, rarely meets other bears, and disappears into a den for months at a time in the winter. What is life really like for a brown bear? How does it spend its days? What are its favorite pastimes? What happens when two bears meet? How does it raise its young? To find out all about brown bears, we need to enter their secret world.

SECRETS OF SUCCESS

The brown bear has been highly successful in the wild. One of the secrets of its success is that it can live in so many places. Forests are one of their favorite homes, but brown bears can also live well high in the mountains, where trees cannot grow. Bears can live in open grasslands and along sea coasts. They can also survive in areas that are almost as dry as deserts. They can thrive in the cold, dry arctic tundra.

Brown bears from all over the world are members of the same family, which is known as *Ursus arctos.*

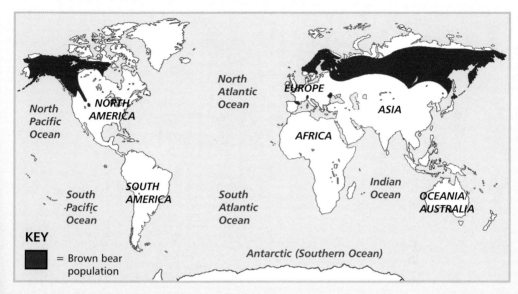

Brown bears can be found in the northern regions of three continents: North America, Europe, and Asia.

Why is the brown bear such a great survivor?
- The brown bear lives on its own, which cuts down on competition for food.
- The brown bear is an **omnivore**, which means it eats all types of foods.
- In the winter, the brown bear can survive five to eight months without eating.
- The brown bear has no natural enemies in the wild.

WHERE DO BROWN BEARS LIVE?

Brown bears roam across three continents: Europe, Asia, and North America. Large bear populations used to roam all three continents, but now bears only live in the northern regions of the world.

Two types of brown bears live in North America. The larger brown bears, known as Kodiak bears, live on Alaska's southern coast and nearby islands. Grizzly bears, named for their silver-gray flecked, or "grizzled," coats, live in Western Canada and in the U.S. states of Alaska, Idaho, Montana, Wyoming, and Washington.

Brown bears' thick, furry coats come in many shades of brown, from cream-colored to almost black. Their faces and shoulders are different than those of another kind of bear, called the black bear, which is common in North America.

5

The Ways of Brown Bears

The brown bear lives alone, without help or support from other living creatures. Even an animal as large and powerful as a brown bear, however, needs a few basic things to survive in the wild.

FINDING A HOME

A brown bear must establish a **home range**, an area where it can live without competing with other bears for food. The size of a bear's range may be as small as 40 square miles (100 square kilometers) or as big as 800 square miles (2,000 sq km), depending on how much food is available. Home ranges often overlap, so that a number of bears can live in the same area. Bears are skilled at keeping out of each other's way. Males, which are called **boars**, usually have larger ranges than females because they need more to eat.

A number of females, which are called **sows**, may live within a boar's range. A boar will search his range for a mate in the breeding season. Females with cubs have the smallest ranges, because the cubs are too small to travel far.

If food is scarce, a bear will need a much larger range in which to fish, find plants to eat, and hunt for meat.

FINDING FOOD

Nothing is more important to a brown bear than food. The brown bear is a great hunter. It can pull down an animal as big as a moose or swat an animal that is as small as a squirrel. Hunting animals, however, takes a lot of energy and is not always successful. Because hunting is not easy, brown bears have broadened their tastes so they can eat all types of food. They will eat plants, such as grasses, sedges, roots, fruit, pine nuts, ripe berries, and even moss.

Brown bears are experts at fishing for salmon and other fish. They wade right into the water to scoop them up. They will also eat **carrion**, which is the rotting bodies of animals that have died in the wild. Their hunting, fishing, and plant-gathering skills bring healthy variety to their diet.

A bear's home range contains a number of different animals and plants that the bear hunts and gathers for food, depending on the time of year. Brown bears will track herds of elk, deer, or caribou in the spring, when bear cubs are being born. Bears will travel to rivers where salmon **spawn** in the late summer, and they will visit mountain meadows that have good crops of berries in the fall.

A BREEDING PARTNER

Male and female brown bears must find each other during the breeding season to create new generations of bears that will keep the **species** alive. Sows are only available for breeding every three to five years, after they have raised their cubs. Boars must often travel long distances to find a partner whose cubs are grown and is ready to breed again.

The only time adult brown bears come close to one another is in the breeding season.

7

The Brown Bear's Perfect Body

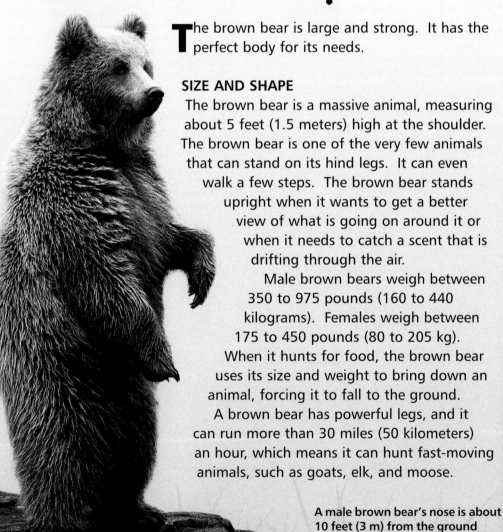

The brown bear is large and strong. It has the perfect body for its needs.

SIZE AND SHAPE

The brown bear is a massive animal, measuring about 5 feet (1.5 meters) high at the shoulder. The brown bear is one of the very few animals that can stand on its hind legs. It can even walk a few steps. The brown bear stands upright when it wants to get a better view of what is going on around it or when it needs to catch a scent that is drifting through the air.

Male brown bears weigh between 350 to 975 pounds (160 to 440 kilograms). Females weigh between 175 to 450 pounds (80 to 205 kg).

When it hunts for food, the brown bear uses its size and weight to bring down an animal, forcing it to fall to the ground.

A brown bear has powerful legs, and it can run more than 30 miles (50 kilometers) an hour, which means it can hunt fast-moving animals, such as goats, elk, and moose.

A male brown bear's nose is about 10 feet (3 m) from the ground when it stands upright — ideal for picking up scents.

Bears that live on the coast have a constant supply of **high-protein** fish. This protein helps them grow much bigger than bears that live inland. Bears that live away from waters with good fishing tend to eat more plants and less protein.

MUSCLE POWER

A brown bear can break the spine of a bison with a single blow. It is strong enough to move huge rocks when searching for food.

A brown bear's great strength is in its front legs and shoulders. The power comes from a hump of muscle across the bear's shoulders. Black bears do not have this hump of muscle.

Brown bears will often hide their food and return to it later. A brown bear was once seen dragging the body of a 1,000-pound (454-kg) elk one-half mile up a steep hill to find a hiding place.

CLAWS

The brown bear's legs end in massive paws, each of which are tipped with five extremely powerful claws. The claws of a brown bear can be up to six inches (15 centimenters) long. Unlike other meat-eating hunters, such

The brown bear has huge canine teeth, which are 2 inches (5 cm) long, on its upper and lower jaws.

as lions and tigers, the brown bear cannot pull its claws in. The bears' claws get rubbed smooth as they walk, so their claws are less sharp than the claws of the big cats. The brown bear's claws may not be extremely sharp, but they work well for digging.

TEETH

A brown bear's teeth are made to eat any kind of food. A bear uses its **canine teeth** to grab on to its **prey** and kill it. It uses its **molars** and **premolars** for grinding and chewing plants and meat.

COAT

The brown bear has a very thick fur coat, which helps to keep it warm during the winter months.

How a Brown Bear Sees the World

Imagine yourself in the huge body of a brown bear, and find out how the world feels to you. How well can you see? How well can you hear?

EYESIGHT

A brown bear has a large head, but its eyes are small. People used to think that bears had poor eyesight. In fact, the brown bear has fairly good vision, but it is nearsighted. A bear needs to come up close to inspect an object, and it has trouble seeing at a distance. Brown bears can see in color. They are at their most active at dawn and at dusk, which shows that they can hunt and find plants to eat in dim light.

The brown bear gets much of the important information it needs by using its nose.

A brown bear uses its nose to find rodents deep underground, and it can even locate food supplies that have been buried by small animals, such as pocket gophers.

HEARING

The brown bear has excellent hearing. Like a dog, it can hear high-pitched sounds that humans cannot hear. This ability helps bears hear and hunt small animals, such as gophers and ground squirrels, that live in burrows underground.

SMELL

The brown bear has an amazing sense of smell, which is rated as one of the best in the animal kingdom. A brown bear's sense of smell is so good that it can detect human scent fourteen hours after a person has passed along a trail. A sense of smell is much more important to a bear than its hearing or eyesight.

The brown bear uses its nose in the following ways:

- to find food (a bear will follow the scent trail of an animal for several miles)
- to find a partner in the breeding season
- to keep away from other bears, and also to keep clear of people

11

Discovering Special Skills

The brown bear has the body of a hunter, but 90 percent of its diet is vegetarian. The brown bear is a great **forager**. Bears have developed special skills so that they can make use of every type of food they find.

FORAGING

There is no food that a bear does not think of as a tasty snack. A brown bear is a very curious animal. It investigates everything it comes across in the hope that it is something good to eat. Bears are also good at solving problems, and they can figure out how to get at food even when it is buried underground or hidden by rocks. A bear will even break into a car when it is searching for food!

The bear also has a remarkably good memory, which is a great help when it needs to find food. When a bear discovers a good food supply, it returns to the same spot year after year, remembering where to find the food and at what time of the year it is available.

DIGGING

Brown bears use their powerful front legs and their long claws for digging. The brown bear digs intently, sometimes for thirty

A bear will use every chance it gets to find food, even if it means getting wet and cold.

Got it! After a patient wait, this brown bear catches a fish, using its paws and its mouth.

minutes at a time, moving large mounds of earth to reach the underground burrow of a ground squirrel or a gopher. A bear will also dig deep underground to find roots and insect nests. The brown bear is an expert at using its claws to tear open rotting logs to find ant nests. Bears enjoy eating ants!

FISHING AND SWIMMING
The brown bear is a champion fisher. When they are fishing for salmon, brown bears give up their solitary ways and fish alongside each other. In the late summer,

when salmon swim upstream to lay their eggs, bears gather along the riverbank and show off their skills.

Bears are also good swimmers. Some bears will stand on the bank and catch the passing fish with their paws. Others wait patiently in the water and swim with powerful strokes to catch fish in their mouths. Some bears even duck their heads underwater so they can get a better view of the fish when they swim past. The most spectacular bear-fishers are those that catch salmon in midair as the fish leap out of the water.

What Does a Brown Bear Do All Day?

The brown bear is a shy, secretive animal that keeps well hidden. Scientists have spent long periods tracking and studying bears to find out how they spend their time.

FEEDING

Brown bears are most active early in the morning and in the evening. At these times of day, a brown bear hunts or forages for food. Finding enough food is a priority for all wild animals, but it is especially important for the brown bear. During the summer months, when food is plentiful, a bear must eat as much as possible. It needs to build up enough fat to live off during the winter, when it may go for five to eight months without eating as it sleeps through the coldest months of the year.

ON PATROL

A brown bear marks its home range to show other bears that

Some brown bears make a special journey to Yellowstone National Park in the summer so they can feast on cutworm moths. A bear may eat 20,000 moths in a day.

After a big meal, a brown bear likes to rest.

the area is already taken. The bear does this by scraping and rubbing against trees and other **landmarks** in its territory. Marking is a way of saying: "This range belongs to me. No visitors are welcome." Its marks warn other bears to stay away.

TRAVELING
The brown bear is a great traveler. It may walk for hundreds of miles (kilometers) to find the best food supply. A bear knows every part of its territory and remembers the best route to take when it goes after a certain type of food. These routes are known as travel corridors. A boar also travels to find a sow during the breeding season.

Scientists have discovered that brown bears have a remarkable ability to find their way home. They have observed a bear that was removed from its range and then released more than 125 miles (200 km) away. The bear was able to find its way back to its range.

RESTING
Brown bears usually rest in the middle of the day. Most bears know of a number of sheltered resting places scattered across their ranges. A bear may relax under a tree or against a rock. Sometimes, it will scrape the earth to make a shallow bed for itself where it can sleep during the day.

15

How Brown Bears Communicate

Brown bears like to keep out of each other's way. Sometimes, however, they need to communicate with one another.

SECRET SIGNS
Bears try to avoid actual meetings. They usually are able to smell if a bear is nearby, and then they will take another route, if necessary. Brown bears leave secret scent messages for each other, which only other bears can understand.

MOANS AND ROARS
The solitary brown bear has no need to "talk" to other bears on a regular basis and so it rarely uses its voice. When a bear is foraging for food, it makes a low moaning sound. For the rest of the day, a brown bear is silent, unless it senses that another bear has come into its range. Then, the brown bear makes a great booming roar, warning all bears in the neighborhood to keep away. If rival males meet, they will growl fiercely at each other.

WOOFS AND WHIMPERS
A mother with cubs has a great need to talk. She snorts to call her cubs to follow her. She uses scolding growls to tell them off and loud woofs to warn them of danger. Cubs also

A brown bear is quick to sense if another bear has come visiting. It may use its voice to warn the stranger to stay away.

The biggest, most powerful bears claim the best fishing sites and growl fiercely if another bear gets too close.

need to talk to their mother to tell her how they are feeling. A cub whines or whimpers when it is hurt or stuck. It hisses when it is frightened, and it makes a little humming sound when it is taking milk from its mother or when it is sleepy and contented.

GROUP MEETINGS

The brown bear breaks its own rules about living alone when it finds plenty of food around. At the McNeil River in Alaska, for example, as many as sixty bears have been seen fishing together. These group meetings can cause problems for bears. Bears are not used to being close to each other and competing for food, so they can be drawn into fighting when they get together.

Usually, they make each other keep a safe distance from one another. Often, the larger bears will claim the best fishing sites. A bear looks as ferocious as possible to warn other bears to keep away. It will flatten its ears, open its mouth, and raise its snout. Then it makes a growl or bellows an ear-splitting roar, which will drive other bears away without needing to fight.

Times of Trouble

One secret of survival is to keep out of trouble. Even an animal as powerful as a bear usually prefers not to fight. If a bear gets injured in a fight, it can be disastrous. The wound can get infected, and the infection can kill the bear. Another danger with injuries is that when a bear is too weak to find food, it can starve to death before it heals.

FIGHTING BEARS

Brown bears have found ways of avoiding each other, and fights between bears are rare. When groups of bears gather around a plentiful supply of food, they may get into disputes, but these are

The brown bear will appear as scary as possible to drive off a rival bear.

If threats do not work, the two rival bears will be forced to fight each other.

usually settled without a fight or even any physical contact.

The real danger comes when two **rival** boars meet while they are looking for a sow that is ready for breeding. The bears threaten each other, hoping that one will give in. If this does not happen, the bigger, stronger bear charges on all fours. If the rival male does not run away, there will be a fight.

When they do fight, bears use their powerful front legs and their sharp claws. They also try to bite each other with their sharp teeth and powerful jaws. Sometimes, a fight ends in the death of one of the bears. More often, a bear will only be injured, and it will give in to the stronger bear.

OLD AGE

A brown bear usually lives for twenty to twenty-five years. Bears in zoos live much longer because they do not have to find their own food. Life in the wild is tough for an old bear. It will gradually lose its strength and find it harder to hunt. A bear needs to travel long distances to find food, and this becomes difficult for older bears. A bear must build up enough fat reserves to live off during the winter months. When a bear cannot do this, it will die.

19

When Brown Bears Are Ready to Breed

For a period of about four weeks in June, everything changes in the bear world. Instead of keeping out of each other's way, boars and sows who are ready to breed actively seek out one another.

BREEDING SEASON

A sow is ready for breeding when she is five years old. A boar may be a couple of years older before he has found his own home range and is ready to compete with other males to find a female.

When a sow wants to attract a boar, she leaves scent messages around her range. She may also roar to tell boars in the area that she is available for breeding. A boar travels long distances, constantly stopping to "read" scent messages as he searches for a partner. Because a sow will not accept a boar when she is raising

A boar must be able to travel long distances to find a female to breed with.

For a few brief days, a boar and a sow bear will live together, and then the boar will return to his home range.

her cubs, she is only available for breeding every three to five years. This limit makes the boar's task of finding a partner much harder. It is also the main reason that bear populations increase very slowly.

When a boar and a sow meet to breed, the boar attracts the sow with low snorts, and he will often nibble her on the neck.

After a brief **courtship**, the pair will **mate**. They spend ten to twelve days together. After this period of time, the boar goes back to his range. He takes no further interest in the sow or the cubs that she gives birth to. He will live alone until the next breeding season.

PREGNANT SOWS

A **pregnant** sow does not change shape for some months, because the cubs do not start to grow big inside her very quickly. She can still go on with her daily routines, hunting, fishing, and foraging for food. While all bears need to build up fat in the summer, it is even more important that a pregnant sow finds plenty to eat, because she gives birth to her cubs in the depths of winter when no food is available.

A pregnant sow digs a den, or burrow, in the ground in the late fall. Then, inside the den, she prepares an area where she will give birth to her cubs.

21

Bears That Sleep All Winter

The brown bear has found the perfect solution to the cold winter — sleep right through it! In late October, in the northern part of the world, the temperature drops, and food becomes scarce. Instead of struggling to keep warm and hunt, the brown bear sleeps in a den until the spring. This special, long sleep is called **hibernation**.

PREPARATIONS

In the last few weeks of summer, brown bears spend all their time eating. They must pile on the pounds so that they build up the fat reserves that will allow them to live through the winter months without eating. During the last weeks of summer, a bear forages for food almost nonstop, with just a few short rest periods. During this time, a bear may eat up to eighty pounds (36 kg) of food in a single day.

BUILDING A DEN

A brown bear uses its great digging skills to build a deep den, which will keep out the very worst

When the first snow comes, food becomes scarce, and so it is time for the bear to hibernate, or sleep.

The brown bear's thick fur helps keep it warm during its long winter sleep.

of the weather. The best place for a den is on a sheltered slope, either among the roots of a tree or next to a large rock. A bear digs deep into the earth. Both boars and sows build dens that have three main parts:

- the entrance hole, which is just big enough for a bear to squeeze through
- a short passage that leads to a sleeping area
- the "bedroom," which is slightly bigger than the bear and is lined with dry plants and grass

Sometimes, a bear will return to the same den year after year, but in most cases, a bear will build a fresh new den every year.

THE BIG SLEEP

A bear is the only **mammal** in the animal kingdom that can go for half the year without eating, drinking, or relieving itself of bodily waste.

The bear enters its den, usually after the first snowfall, and goes into a state of hibernation. In this state, the bear's temperature drops a few degrees below normal, and its heartbeat and breathing slow down. The bear is in a drowsy, sleepy state, using as little energy as possible.

A hibernating bear is not in a deep sleep and will wake up very easily. When the snow starts to melt in March, the bear wakes up and comes out of its den.

23

The Family Life of Brown Bears

You might think it is tough for a bear to survive all winter without eating. What about the pregnant sows that give birth and feed their cubs without getting a scrap of food for themselves?

NEWBORN CUBS

A sow gives birth to her cubs in January or February. She usually has twins, but she may have as many as four cubs in a litter. Her cubs are completely helpless when they are born, and they weigh no more than 1.5 pounds (.68 kg), which is only about 1 percent of their mother's weight. The cubs have no fur, and they are blind and toothless. All they can do is drink milk from their mother.

For the next couple of months, the mother remains in her drowsy state while the cubs nurse. The milk she produces is rich in **nutrients**, which means the cubs grow very fast. The milk has a fat

The cubs follow close behind their mother. If she warns them of danger, they will scramble up the nearest tree. Adult bears are too big and heavy to climb trees.

To begin with, the bear cubs watch their mother fishing for salmon before they try to fish by themselves.

content of 20 percent, compared with 4 percent fat in human milk.

LEAVING THE DEN
Adult brown bears come out of their dens in March, but a mother with newborn cubs waits a little longer to give her babies a chance to grow. By the time the cubs come out of the den in April, they weigh around 50 to 60 pounds (23 to 27 kg).

By this time, the mother bear is very hungry. She has had to wait an extra month or more before eating after her long winter's sleep. She will have lost a huge amount of weight while giving birth and **nursing** her cubs. The mother may have lost up to 40 percent of her body weight.

While the cubs explore the outside world for the first time, the mother must look after them, but she must also concentrate on eating. She needs to get back the weight she has lost. She continues to feed the cubs until they are five months old, so she is not just hunting and fishing for herself.

The Bear Cubs Grow Up

Brown bears are devoted mothers, caring for their cubs from birth until they are at least three years old. During this time, a mother does everything she can for her cubs. She feeds them, shows them how to hunt and forage for food, and protects them from danger.

In spite of all her care, only half the cubs born survive to become adults. Cubs may be killed by wolves, lack of food, or even by violent weather.

LEARNING THROUGH PLAY
As the cubs get bigger, they become more and more playful. They roll around and wrestle together, and they will chase each other and play-fight. The cubs are having fun, but they are also

These two youngsters are having a play-fight, preparing themselves for life in the adult world.

learning how to use their bodies so they can hunt and fight when they need to.

By the time they are eight months old, the cubs are eating solid foods, including berries, nuts, roots, grasses, fish, and meat. The mother travels around her range, showing her cubs the best places to find food. At this stage, the mother does not catch food for her cubs. She keeps the food for herself, and the cubs, driven by hunger, try to snatch bites. This teaches them to compete for food.

The cubs stay with their mother for at least three years, living in the den with her in the winter. The young bears watch their mother and learn how to hunt, fish, graze on plants, and dig for food.

A young bear will be able to take care of itself when it is around three years old.

GOING SOLO

When a mother bear is ready to breed again, she drives her cubs away. By this time, the cubs are three to four years old. They are able to hunt and fish by themselves. For their first summer and winter, brothers and sisters will stay together and share a den. In the spring, the young bears separate and search for a range of their own.

In many cases, the young bears find a range that is within their mother's range, or close to it. The young bears already have a good knowledge of the area and they will remember all the places where their mother took them to feed.

Brown Bears and People

Brown bears have lived on Earth for many thousands of years, with no enemies to fear. Now, human beings pose the greatest danger to their survival. In the 1800s, more than 100,000 brown bears lived in North America. Today, fewer than 1,000 roam free in the lower forty-eight states, where they are considered an **endangered species**. The state of Alaska has a brown bear population of about 30,000.

EARLY SETTLERS

After the first European settlers came to North America, they began moving west in the eighteenth century. They were eager to tame the new country. They set to work clearing the land for farming and building homes and roads. They started to keep large herds of cattle.

The brown bear was feared and often hated by North American settlers.

Special trips are now organized so that people can see brown bears living in the wild.

Brown bears no longer had the land to themselves, but they were quick to seize on the benefits. Cattle proved to be easy prey. The bears also learned that where there are people, there is garbage. Raiding the garbage dump is another way of finding an easy meal. In no time, brown bears were considered a major nuisance and thousands were shot. Another danger for brown bears was hunting. Big game hunting was popular, and the mark of a great huntsman was to shoot a bear.

BEAR ATTACKS

A brown bear does not attack people without reason. If a bear is suddenly disturbed, or if a mother is protecting her cubs, however, a bear may attack. While still rare, the number of bear attacks on people is rising, especially in bear ranges where humans are living or visiting in larger numbers than ever before. In areas where brown bears live, people are warned and told how to behave near them.

A BRIGHTER FUTURE?

Today, we have a better understanding of brown bears. We are finding ways to help them survive. Strong laws protect brown bears, and they are free to roam in huge national parks, such as Yellowstone, the Rocky Mountains, and the North Cascades.

The greatest danger that bears face is losing places to live. Their **wilderness** areas are disappearing. It is vital that we find areas where the brown bear can live in safety. Otherwise, this mighty animal will be lost forever.

Glossary

boar a male bear

canine teeth the sharpest teeth, used for biting and killing

carrion the rotting body of a dead animal

courtship when two animals convince one another to mate

endangered species any group of animals that is officially at risk of becoming extinct. These groups are protected from hunters, trappers, and loss of habitat by laws and international treaties.

forager an animal that searches for food

hibernation when an animal rests in a sleep state for months at a time, slowing down its breathing and other body functions so that it uses up as little energy as possible

high-protein rich in protein, a very valuable source of food

home range an area of land where a bear lives

landmarks features, such as rocks, that stand out and are easy to spot

mammal any of the family of furry, warm-blooded, milk-producing animals that give birth to live young

mate when two animals breed together to make babies

molars teeth used for grinding and chewing

nursing when cubs or other baby mammals feed by sucking milk from their mothers

nutrients substances in food that provide necessary elements for healthy bodies (in this case, helping bear cubs to grow).

omnivore an animal that eats everything, from plants to fish and meat

pregnant a female animal who is carrying a baby or babies inside

premolars teeth used for grinding and chewing

prey animals that are hunted by meat-eaters

rival one who competes for territory, mates, or power

sow a female bear

spawn when fish lay eggs

species a group of animals that are similar to each other

wilderness a place where wild animals live without people

More Books to Read

Brown Bear. Read and Learn (series). Patricia Whitehouse (Heinemann)

The Grizzly Bear. Endangered and Threatened Animals (series). Lisa Harkrader (Enslow)

Grizzly Bears. Predators in the Wild (series). Kathleen W. Deady (Edge Books)

Grizzly Bears. Untamed World (series). Janice Parker (Steck-Vaughn).

Grizzly Bears. Wild Bears (series). Jason and Jody Stone. (Blackbirch Press)

Web Sites

Grizzlies at National Wildlife Federation
www.nwf.org/grizzlybear/

Grizzly Bear Quiz
www.bccf.com/ecoed/Kids/griz_q.html

Grizzly Photos
www.bear.org/Grizzly/Grizzly_Photo_Gallery_1.html

Kids Bear Dialogue
www.idahoptv.org/dialogue4kids/bears/facts.html

National Geographic for Kids
www.nationalgeographic.com/kids/creature_feature/0010/
brownbears.html

Publisher's note to educators and parents: Our editors have carefully reviewed these Web sites to ensure that they are suitable for children. Many Web sites change frequently, however, and we cannot guarantee that a site's future contents will continue to meet our high standards of quality and educational value. Be advised that children should be closely supervised whenever they access the Internet.

Index